Creating Your
Custom Kitchen

Tina Skinner

4880 Lower Valley Road Atglen, Pennsylvania 19310

Schiffer Books are available at special discounts for bulk purchases for sales promotions or premiums. Special editions, including personalized covers, corporate imprints, and excerpts can be created in large quantities for special needs. For more information contact the publisher:

Published by Schiffer Publishing Ltd.
4880 Lower Valley Road
Atglen, PA 19310
Phone: (610) 593-1777; Fax: (610) 593-2002
E-mail: Info@schifferbooks.com

For the largest selection of fine reference books on this and related subjects, please visit our web site at:
www.schifferbooks.com
We are always looking for people to write books on new and related subjects. If you have an idea for a book please contact us at the above address.

This book may be purchased from the publisher.
Include $5.00 for shipping.
Please try your bookstore first.
You may write for a free catalog.

In Europe, Schiffer books are distributed by
Bushwood Books
6 Marksbury Ave.
Kew Gardens
Surrey TW9 4JF England
Phone: 44 (0) 20 8392-8585; Fax: 44 (0) 20 8392-9876
E-mail: info@bushwoodbooks.co.uk
Website: www.bushwoodbooks.co.uk
Free postage in the U.K., Europe; air mail at cost.

Acknowledgements

Among the many, credit goes to Ginger Doyle, Photo Editor, Dinah Roseberry, Copy Editor, and Sherry Qualls and Caitlin Jacobson of White Good & Co. Advertising who worked to make everything take place seamlessly.

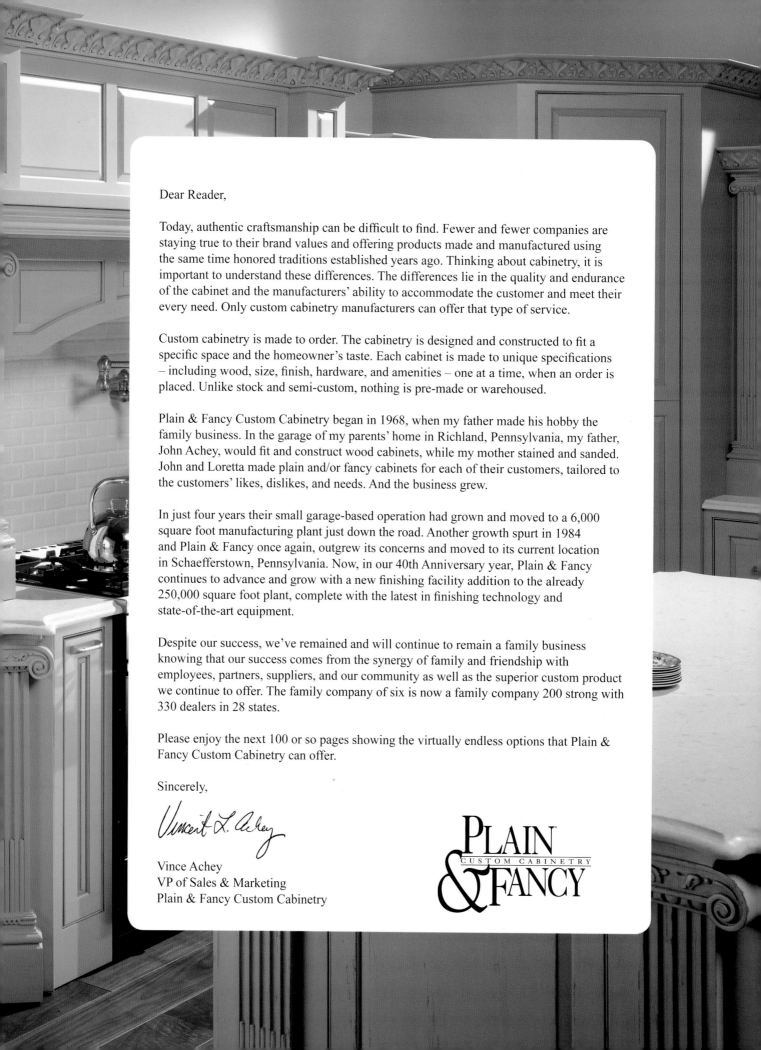

Dear Reader,

Today, authentic craftsmanship can be difficult to find. Fewer and fewer companies are staying true to their brand values and offering products made and manufactured using the same time honored traditions established years ago. Thinking about cabinetry, it is important to understand these differences. The differences lie in the quality and endurance of the cabinet and the manufacturers' ability to accommodate the customer and meet their every need. Only custom cabinetry manufacturers can offer that type of service.

Custom cabinetry is made to order. The cabinetry is designed and constructed to fit a specific space and the homeowner's taste. Each cabinet is made to unique specifications – including wood, size, finish, hardware, and amenities – one at a time, when an order is placed. Unlike stock and semi-custom, nothing is pre-made or warehoused.

Plain & Fancy Custom Cabinetry began in 1968, when my father made his hobby the family business. In the garage of my parents' home in Richland, Pennsylvania, my father, John Achey, would fit and construct wood cabinets, while my mother stained and sanded. John and Loretta made plain and/or fancy cabinets for each of their customers, tailored to the customers' likes, dislikes, and needs. And the business grew.

In just four years their small garage-based operation had grown and moved to a 6,000 square foot manufacturing plant just down the road. Another growth spurt in 1984 and Plain & Fancy once again, outgrew its concerns and moved to its current location in Schaefferstown, Pennsylvania. Now, in our 40th Anniversary year, Plain & Fancy continues to advance and grow with a new finishing facility addition to the already 250,000 square foot plant, complete with the latest in finishing technology and state-of-the-art equipment.

Despite our success, we've remained and will continue to remain a family business knowing that our success comes from the synergy of family and friendship with employees, partners, suppliers, and our community as well as the superior custom product we continue to offer. The family company of six is now a family company 200 strong with 330 dealers in 28 states.

Please enjoy the next 100 or so pages showing the virtually endless options that Plain & Fancy Custom Cabinetry can offer.

Sincerely,

Vince Achey
VP of Sales & Marketing
Plain & Fancy Custom Cabinetry

PLAIN &FANCY
CUSTOM CABINETRY

Table of Contents

Introduction 6

Unique Storage 8

Built-Ins 16

Free-Standing Furniture 18

Arts & Crafts Style 20

Cooking Up Contemporary 24

Old-World Charm 42

Country Classics 52

Home Away from Home 64

Keeping it Colorful 70

We Love White 82

Rustic Recipes 88

Sticking to Tradition 92

Bars and Beverage Stations............................. 106

Other Rooms 108

Introduction

With custom, almost anything is possible. Custom offers the versatility of freestanding accent pieces and furniture, as well as fitted cabinets. You can choose a door style that suits your taste, be it contemporary or classic, and have it made in the wood species that speaks to you: Cherry, Pine, Walnut, Maple, and Oak. There are dozens of wonderful finishes to choose, from soft antique-distressed to stylish low-sheen or custom-colored enamels, as well as traditional stains ranging from rich and dark to pale, natural tones. Retailers and designers will also talk about semi-custom cabinets, which are mid-priced, but offer a fair amount of flexibility. Many of the components are stock, but they have features that help the kitchen designer achieve a near-custom fit. Stock offers the least versatility, but the most affordability. You'll find you need to match up stock parts, typically a modular system, to your kitchen space, and things won't always fit to maximize space and storage.

What makes a custom kitchen worth the extra price and a deeper investment in thought and time, is the benefit of the "yours only" factor. Custom cabinetry is built to your exact specifications – color, door style, wood species, and finish. Cabinet height and depth can be adjusted to fit corners and unusually shaped spaces. Moreover, potential "dead space" can be creatively turned into a unique storage areas, for the best look and optimum use of every nook and cranny. You can have a kitchen that's one and only. Yours. And you should.

Today you can walk into a home-improvement store and order stock cabinetry right off the showroom floor, and probably arrange for a contractor to come and install it. This is the rock-bottom way to redo a kitchen, and the most attractive if you're getting ready to "flip" your house, or rent out your condo. If you're planning to live with the cabinetry, however, you might want to put more thought and individuality into the kitchen you design and install.

For anyone considering a kitchen renovation, the following are important points to consider:

1. Consult a kitchen designer

Kitchen design is highly specialized. If you're working with an architect and/or an interior designer, insist on working with a kitchen designer as well to ensure a well-planned, well-executed design. And involve the kitchen designer early in the process, whether you're building or remodeling.

Kitchen designers understand how a kitchen works. They think about the little things that can become big if not anticipated – like the placement of outlets, size and shape of appliances, and proper storage spaces. They know about kitchen trends, innovations, and specific manufacturer details; they keep abreast of the frequent changes, custom finishes and options offered by many companies that will be a part of your dream kitchen.

Think of your kitchen designer as your advocate, who adds value by providing knowledge and ideas. Engaging one is not only helpful, but inspirational and smart. A kitchen designer is worth the investment.

2. Zone planning

A properly planned kitchen shortens the distances between spaces allocated for different purposes, or zones, within the kitchen.

Zone for consumables
First and foremost, a kitchen is about food. Traditionally, the important "stock" in a kitchen includes sugar, flour, coffee, and other durable items such as pasta, bread, canned goods, and cereal. A refrigerator brings perishable goods into the kitchen, such as milk, eggs, fruits, and vegetables.

Zone for non-consumables
Non-consumables in the kitchen includes kitchen utensils, cutlery, plastic containers, and those seldom used small appliances that are tucked away until they're needed. These items will likely account for a third of the items stored in your kitchen, and you want to plan for easy access in lower and upper cabinets.

Zones for cleaning
A "wet" area of the kitchen accounts for the sink and dishwasher. Cleaning tools and detergents are generally stored close at hand to the wet areas. This zone or zones will also include trash bags, tea towels, and waste and recycling bins.

Zone for preparation

This zone contains the main work areas of the kitchen. You'll want this area to be well lit, and of sufficient size. This is where you'll store the bulk of your kitchen utensils and tools, small appliances, spices, cooking oils, and sauces, and anything else that is frequently used in preparing food.

Zone for cooking

The heart of every kitchen, this is where the stove, range, microwave and all the pots, pans, trays, and items used in cooking should be kept close at hand.

3. Design compartmentally for good flow

Collections, place settings, and glassware don't belong where you cook. Spices and cookware do. Designate storage space for tabletop items away from your cooking areas, so the "chef" doesn't collide with those setting the table or making cocktails.

4. Give dry goods a proper home – a pantry

Our forefathers were right. A "dry refrigerator" is invaluable. Dry goods need a cool, dark, and dry place. A pantry fits the bill. Only remember that today, we, unlike the pilgrims, have electricity. A pantry with no lighting equals a dark cavern. Make sure to include adjustable shelves and wire baskets for onions and other root vegetables as well.

5. Make lighting a priority

Don't skimp on integrating good task lighting everywhere you work. Halogen is popular, or choose more conventional spot lighting.

6. Think about you and your things

Particularly with custom, you can design a perfect kitchen for you and all you've acquired. Take stock and make sure your design accommodates your belongings. Renovation can be overwhelming, but when it's all over, that space should speak to who you are, what you need, and where.

7. Question open shelving or glass-front cabinets

These two design elements are indisputably pretty, but unless you love to dust shelving and wash windows, be careful.

8. Contemplate the trash

Make sure your trash and recycling center is hidden behind cabinetry and close to a door leading outside.

You may be surprised to learn that custom doesn't have to break the bank. For avid cooks in remodeling mode, a custom kitchen is a smart investment. Not only will it make life easier in your kitchen, but a well-designed, quality kitchen adds considerable value to your home.

Custom cabinetry pricing varies widely and can be affected by the size of your kitchen, wood species, finish choice, door style, and other variables. A kitchen designer can help you ballpark prices as part of an initial consultation. When moving forward with your kitchen, the designer will typically charge a design fee, which is often put towards the cost of cabinetry when the kitchen is ordered. But do keep in mind that Plain & Fancy Custom Cabinetry can be surprisingly affordable.

The images in this book were drawn from the collection of Plain & Fancy Custom Cabinetry, a family-owned cabinetmaker located in Schaefferstown, Pennsylvania. Every cabinet shown was built with one of two time-tested methods: framed, mortise, and tenon construction with dovetail drawers; or full access (frameless) dowel construction, also with dovetail drawers. Each one is the pride and joy of an owner, and unique only to their house. However, it's hoped that what inspired them will also launch your own ideas for how to create a kitchen that is uniquely you. For more information on custom cabinetry please visit ww.plainfancycabinetry.com.

Unique Storage

Opposite page:
Solid wood utensil drawer with clever cutouts and built-in sliding top drawer is a neat nesting place, designed to fit individual cutlery pieces.

Sliding drawers within a drawer add storage options and supreme organization.

Here, stovetop and baking cutlery is stored atop a deep drawer of corresponding cookware like pots and frying pans.

An under-sink drawer was custom-configured to accommodate plumbing and keep cleaning tools organized.

Counterclockwise from top:
Doors conceal an undersink pull-out feature that makes this a "cleaner cabinet" in more ways than one.

Apothecary drawers under the range provide at-hand storage.

Spice drawers with a unique bottle-bracing design and a pull-out under a range.

11

A step stool allows youngsters to help at the counter.

A pull-out cutting board provides prep space for a chef's helpers.

A dog's dinner is smartly concealed below the counter, out of tipping-over, and tripping-over, reach.

A dual-drawer dishwasher is cleverly concealed.

A deep drawer is perfect for storing root vegetables.

Above left:
A breadbox with clear plastic top helps preserve freshness and retain visibility.

Garbage bags and bottled beverages find a home in a utility drawer.

A pull-out pot rack brings cookware into the light.

A pull-out drawer makes the best use of corner space, perfect for narrow, tall bottles.

This swing-out pantry brings its contents forward as it opens, so you don't have to hunt in the back or sacrifice inner door storage.

This shallow stove drawer sits just below the range to keep the essentials at hand.

Built-Ins

Left:
This arts-and-crafts armoire, built into a wall of complementary cabinetry, features coordinating faux-pane doors and matching knobs, but a slightly different finish commands attention.

An armoire fills a niche and provides beautiful display area and storage.

Built-in display shelves create an attractive wall.

Free-Standing Furniture

This free-standing piece is full of spirit – literally!
A wine rack and elegant stemware rack sidle up
to a small wet bar, and below, a cooler keeps
beverages chilled and ready.

A cranberry-colored hutch features a plate
rack at eye-level, open shelving above and
cabinets below, with a handy butcher-block
counter surface and five apothecary drawers.

A deep hutch with long open shelving is a great place to prop up pottery and other collections.

Above, left:
This freestanding white hutch might as well be an installation piece, with its column motif giving it such commanding presence. Ample storage is found within many drawers and elegant glass-front cabinets, while an open center console displays the family heirlooms.

A charming table features tiny drawers for organized, specific storage.

Arts & Crafts Style

Dual freestanding workstations complete the color scheme in this kitchen by coordinating, not matching, their snazzy fennel-green and deep mahogany finishes.

A storage armoire features doors fronted with fennel finished woven panels.

A pantry reveals gliding shelves that inch forward as the door swings open, bringing goods into the light.

Open corner shelves, a "thoroughfare" and pass-through give a comfortable, contemporary slant to this oh-so-smart space. Granite countertops lead busy chefs in, while hungry (and thirsty) visitors can wait comfortably at the bar.

A view from the cook's corner shows an array of appliances within easy reach.

Plenty of pass-through space makes for an accessible kitchen. Light gleams through the open channel and illuminates.

Cooking Up Contemporary

Above and top center:
Maple warms the gray tones of countertop, burnished nickel
hardware, and stainless steel appliances. A huge peninsula
seats eight at an elevated granite surface, backed by a wealth
of soapstone at work surface height.

Frosted glass cabinet doors allow a hint of color to shine through. The glass countertop makes for a glistening work surface.

A butcher-block countertop on an open island leaves more room for prep – in this case, for juicing oranges and serving up fresh-squeezed refreshments.

"Tall, thin, and beautiful" doesn't just describe the woman who calls this kitchen her own. With coppery cabinets that seem to reach upward forever, the space that has always existed high above the counter is reclaimed for storage.

Appliances are built right into the wall. Double wall ovens and a refrigerator with matching wood panels frame a television console above cabinets and drawers, with not a single inch wasted.

This small, corner kitchen features a green granite counter, perched atop honey cabinets with stainless steel details; a truly contemporary combination.

Deep, concealed storage is found in this unique unit of beveled glass and solid wood.

A desk attached to the kitchen occurs right at the window – clearly planned by the person who will get to work there.

See large pots easily in this deep drawer beneath the range.

A corner sink cut right into the granite
supports the clean-lined, contemporary
look. Above, a gliding pull-up door
rises to reveal glasses and pitchers.

A stylish island of square, clean lines features the kitchen sink at counter height above an eating area at dining height.

This angle reveals a chic sideboard for plants or other décor and a double-bowl sink that matches sleek, stainless cabinet hardware.

Nothing says "contemporary" like gadgetry; this kitchen has a TV above an already-cool wine refrigerator, which is just a step away from a professional-series double oven with grill top.

A bar convenient to your kitchen *and* your entertaining space is ideal. Just around the corner from the professional kitchen lies this expansive wet bar complete with under-cabinet wine refrigerator.

Overlooking this contemporary dining table of silvery curvature, glass-front cabinets with interior lighting provide a museum look. Ribbed glass softens the view through the other doors, to conceal everyday dishes.

By design, traffic performs a U-turn around this aerodynamic island. Curved doors conceal an abundance of storage.

This space brings a nearly seamless continuity to contemporary with a dramatic bow-front island topped by a deep, green-gray granite counter. White lamps hang above and simulate the soft light emitted from oversized windows over the sink.

This kitchen is part deep cherry and part shiny stainless, but completely stylish.

Top left: An inglenook for quiet Sunday suppers is built-in and coordinates with the cherry cabinets.

Top: Glass-fronted doors over a beverage bar make for an efficient entertainment center.

Custom cabinetry makes the best use of limited space, carving out more of the corner for additional elbow room, and providing a side cookbook shelf by the stove.

Soft blue beams are suspended above a deep purple and black kitchen with accents of bright white, orange, and pale blue. A convection oven and wine refrigerator are built below the sink for "catering" to guests at the bar-height counter, perched atop a sky-blue tiled backsplash.

Custom built, a Tudor inspired hood holds court above the full oven, flanked by extra tall wall cabinets for maximum storage.

A chef's dream oven is accented by a tile backsplash that pays homage to the room's vibrant colors.

Rennie Mackintosh inspired, black-and-white diamond inlay pattern in the tile floor echoes diamond-motif cabinet hardware in deep wood and square storage solutions on the cabinets and counter. Opaque glass fronts hide cabinet clutter.

This Zen kitchen offers simple style and lots of organization; a perfect balance of form and function.

Right:
Across the room, a professional-series stove is tucked into a wall of perfectly planned cabinets, and an ultra-contemporary range hood reaches skyward.

Opposite page:
A leafy-green backsplash coordinates with the deep green counter and soft blue-green linoleum floor. An extended, rounded, butcher-block work center provides prep space and informal dining, and sliding doors on either side open the hollow island for extra storage without open doors getting in the way of traffic.

Above and right:
Warm wood and speckled green work together in this modern kitchen of squares and rectangles. Sparse but not sterile, this kitchen employs a "pillow door" to bring soft to spartan.

In the corner, a pull-out drawer helps bottles and canisters stay orderly.

Old-World Charm

The homeowners wanted a rustic Italian look to remind them of their frequent travels. A cocoa frost finish on cherry wood cabinetry, granite countertop, and Italian tile backsplash combine for rich, Old-World effect.

Soft maple cabinetry finished in a custom pale yellow, a hand-decorated tile backsplash, a seat-and-eat island with a convenient prep sink, and detailed French accents make this country kitchen truly Continental.

Polished granite tops both the counter and island, reflecting the plentiful light that illuminates this many-windowed space. French farmhouse details, from the glass-fronted cabinet to the special shelf above the sink and double-drawer dishwasher allow for Provencal collectibles to be displayed.

This space presents a unique slant on efficiency, fitting a fridge and freezer under the stairs, as well as a wine rack, microwave and bookshelves.

Picking from the pantry has never been so easy with this stack of deep, roll-out shelves.

Custom cabinetry comes together for a 'new country' kitchen with a blend of Shaker and Quaker doorstyles. Beaded inset doors with sheen Wallingford finish adorn the two-tiered Cherry cabinet, while a Maple island in a creamy custom color has seating room for three or more – as well as space for a prep sink, dishwasher, towel rack, and two waste receptacles.

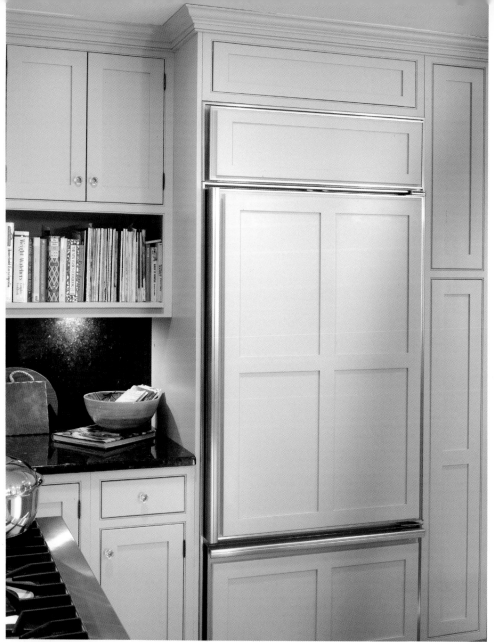

Classic inset doors are matched to
a fridge and freezer inset panel for a
virtually seamless look.

Right:
A Maple keystone arch and leaded
glass-fronted cabinets float astride
a black granite backsplash, pot filler,
and stainless stove, all the better to
bake with.

Far right:
Over the cooktop, a Euro-style
range hood rises above an inlaid tile
diamond design in accents of black,
white, and red.

Above a farmhouse sink, three leaded glass windows let incredible light and views into this charming kitchen. On the wall, three shelves that match the cabinet molding hold potted herbs.

Far left:
For this active family, a kitchen entryway bench with coat hooks, a space for boots, and plenty of storage was essential. Next to it, the refrigerator wears a lovely wooden cabinet that changes its too-contemporary stainless look into a piece of country heirloom furniture.

Left:
A brick-red stove looks stunning between two thin rows of utility and tool drawers with bowed cabinets to the left and right.

This bright, sunny kitchen is a plant-lover's dream-come-true. A skylight and extra deep counter bump out into the sun from the center of a pale green cabinet unit where potting, watering, and pruning can take place. The cooktop is on the center island with large wooden drawers and cabinets below. In the background, a sink and wine cooler work the corner.

In this regal country kitchen, a fluted farmsink is set into a soft tea green cabinet with open shelving to display creamware and glass. On the island, bookshelves and drawers offer even more compartmentalized storage.

Under the sink, caddies keep dishsoap, scrub brushes, and sanitizing sprays from toppling over or getting lost in the dark.

Top left: A pull-out pilaster secretly stores spices.

This aristocratic kitchen celebrates the classics from the scroll-topped pilasters to Greek-inspired moldings. The custom details include the tea green finish coupled wtih a truly special brush mark crackle on the island.

A stunning metal backsplash in ornate floral designs form a grid behind a farm sink set into a counter of black marble flanked by cabinets of creamy beige. Two small sconces intimately light the custom created alcove.

In this historic home, a full wall was replaced with a half wall of walnut cabinetry. The center bump-out takes on the look of a dresser, the perfect foil for a kitchen not trying to be a kitchen.

Far left:
A pull-out shelving unit with Plexiglas® outer braces keeps canisters, boxes of cereal, and other stack-ables in neat rows.

Left:
In the end cabinet, tall dividers keep cookie sheets, cutting boards, and other hard-to-store platters and trays neatly in their own slots.

51

Country Classics

Ultra-tall cabinets reach to the ceiling along this room-divider, while a black counter creates a low horizon line. Hanging a few feet beyond, a pot rack holds copper and black tools that echo the cabinet and counter colors. On the end, a mini-fridge hides behind a wooden panel, accessible to the kitchen *and* living room.

Double ovens are stacked in a tall wall of cabinets across the kitchen. A prep sink does double duty for washing vegetables or filling glasses.

A booth gives this cozy nook an updated look. The house wines are just around the corner, chilling in a cooler with electric temperature control.

Opposite page:
A hutch features a wine cooler below, a china cabinet above, and a small television screen in between for tuning in a favorite cooking program.

Sunlight through large, paned windows sets aglow a yellow kitchen with off-white cabinetry and a mottled green-and-yellow marble counter. Scalloped details, crown moulding and full-overlay Tapestry doors give this space a comfortable and stylish finish. A sloped hood caps the stove and tiled backsplash. Accents of copper, tan, and black appear in pots, drawer pulls, and appliance knobs and keep the eye moving around this sunny space.

A peek into the butler's pantry reveals bold red cabinetry accented by glass fronted doors.

A side door surrounded by efficient storage cabinets leads out to the driveway, where groceries can be marched right into the kitchen.

Traditional does not mean close-minded, especially not in this light, and open area, large enough for a separate island and bar with seating. Arches and high, recessed spaces, paired with tall creamy cabinetry make this conventional-looking space anything but ordinary.

Rows of vertical doors backlight pots hanging high from a custom hood that echoes the island's angles.

Far left:
This kitchen knows when to conceal, and when to show off. The open shelving allows bright copper pots and nesting heart-shaped ceramic baking dishes to work with the warm color scheme.

Left:
With long, subtle arches atop and below, there's a classical sense of symmetry in this built-in maple dresser with curio shelves.

Cabinetry lines the wall with a built-in set of top-of-the-line appliances that fit into their places like puzzle pieces. A beautiful cream-colored island works like a freestanding furniture piece holding books, clay pots, and baskets.

A stately red cabinet was designed to mimic an heirloom antique.

In this kitchen, a suspended cabinet unit replaces a hood over the professional range, for dramatic display of dishes and glasses with interior spotlighting. Below, two can sit at bar-height island to enjoy informal dining that interacts with the busy chef.

White cabinetry makes a country statement, hiding modern appliances behind wood paneling and providing a multitude of storage spaces, including a wall of open-to-the-outdoors shelving. All that white is wisely broken up by fun uses of purples and reds, such as the unique tile backsplash that speaks the language of the fun plaid chairs in the foreground, and the detail of red stove knobs.

Above:
Custom coordinated window shelves are perfect for showing off collectables.

Left:
The specially draped mantle hood is designed to scale the professional range.

An extra long kitchen is cut to size by custom-built arches that soar over sink and stove. Nicely scaled shelves flank the cooking center, all topped by graceful moldings that conquer an abundance of space.

Right:
A deep farmhouse sink is nestled into the washing up nook. Inset cabinets are at home with classic subway tile.

Far right:
Across from the island, a hutch breaks the solid white cabinetry with rich, natural wood finish and granite counter detailing. A vertical plate rack and other unique drawer and cabinet shapes take on the function of a combination furniture, library, secretary area.

This gourmet cook kitchen is equipped with a pastry prep marble topped flip-up, rows of plate racks, and drawers and shelves galore.

Designed for easy access to pots, pans, and plates for plating elegant desserts and festive suppers. The island cooks, rolls, and stores.

The perfect storage solution is a corner pantry, the place to store and be stored.

On the far wall, a large counter perfect for rolling dough or stamping out cookies tops cabinetry that features deep drawers for baking essentials like mixers, cookie sheets, and large bowls.

A warm and welcoming custom country kitchen includes grain bins at the end of the island for all those bulk purchased dry ingredients. The built-in window seats are complete with drawer storage for hats, gloves, and winter woolens. Rooster red cabinets are reminiscent of the barn out back.

Antique distressing gives this kitchen a real French country feeling. Hexagonal stones form the old-world floor under cream-and-caramel cabinets. In lieu of an island, this "monks" table has storage cubbies for napkins, utensils, and candles.

A French "dresser," custom crafted out of fruitwood, provides a perfect place to display antique majolica and copper pots.

Home Away from Home

In a smaller kitchen, moving upward, rather than outward reclaims space. Stacking ovens keep the cooking center compact.

Above right:
Suspended glass-front cabinets, bead board accents, and an abundance of windows keep this kitchen as light and bright as the landscape outside. A beamed ceiling brings a strong presence to the room.

Right:
Look closely: a recessed counter leading to the range top takes advantage of a deep corner and gives helpers that much more room to move about behind the chef. At right, a wide pass-through is perfect to send hot-off-the-stove dishes out to a waiting crowd.

Vintage slant-raised panels create a beautiful dimensional look on this wall of cabinets with a cut-out for a microwave. Built-in shelving at left houses a collection of sun-colored pitchers.

Adjoining the kitchen, two counter-to-ceiling cabinets stand atop a butcher-block counter, with dining area drawers and doors below for linens, delicate dishes, and aprons.

With bead board detailing, a vertical plate rack, and stainless steel appliances, this space could be a waterfront café. A full-overlay vintage doorstyle adorns maple cabinetry, and an inlaid butcher-block top has room for two to dine at the island.

Square has never been so stylish. This cabinetry uses creativity in glass panes to create a block motif, and the island matches with a repeat of the door detail.

Center right:
More squares trace the edges of cube storage, including a custom, geometric wine rack.

Walls made of cabinets form this clean, white kitchen. Horizontal lines are stair-stepped on the island.

A chandelier that draws the eye upward shows off an incredible ceiling of white beams. Shutter cabinet doors echo the ceiling lines, and dark, deep dining furniture, bar stools, and blue island break up the sea of white and anchor the room to its dark wood floor. This beachside kitchen appears to have come straight from Key West.

Bead board makes an unusual and attractive backsplash, with a navy counter top and the cleanest of white cabinets. Simple inset doors integrate dishwasher, drawers, and wine cabinet, all topped off by custom glass fronts.

The backsplash sets the tone in this kitchen of all-natural looks. Fossil fish swim behind the range; natural maple cabinets provide beautiful storage and display. Flip-up storage hidden by frosted glass gives an opaque screen. Open shelves allow for easy access to serving bowls and pitchers from the kitchen or dining area.

A "see through" fridge is trimmed in beaded maple.

A shuttered combination pantry/ freestanding furniture piece keeps the cook's area free for prep.

Keeping it Colorful

Amid limestone counters, a coal-black island, and an aged
barnwood range hood lays a ruddy and rustic kitchen of truly
earth-inspired color, finished with a brave and successful
Rhode Island red. A split counter offers bar-style seating
where diners can absorb the palette.

Beneath a network of rustic beams, this kitchen serves up an eclectic blend of custom colors with antique, distressed details. The space was planned smartly; a warming drawer in the island keeps food cozy; a small silverware drawer holds spoons and other flatware just below the microwave for that stir halfway through a reheating.

Strong crown molding tops this multi-level wall of cabinets. Inset doors give the space a traditional farmhouse look.

The island is full of surprises behind a black cloak of wood paneling. Here, a dishwasher tilts open next to a rinsing sink.

In this kitchen, yellows and warm wood tones take over to create a colorful and spicy kitchen. Dramatic accents of black and red appear in seat cushions, decorative tiles, and bowls, and slim, long silver pulls complement tall cabinets.

The kitchen "desk" is reinvented in this quiet corner.

Color can be found in interesting and unexpected places. An otherwise subdued palette is excited here by red café lighting above the dining table, and echoed in the back wall of a buttercream armoire of colorful dishes spot-lit from within.

Right:
Creamy cabinets with gray and black mottled granite surfaces help the barn-red of accent lighting and backsplash walls to really pop.

Far right:
Above the sink, the wall was left open to display colorful ceramics.

A wall of red efficiently stores dishes, glassware, and serveware. The sink base cabinet offers a beaded inset door in solid black.

A thin utility drawer keeps foils, waxed and parchment papers, and plastic wraps close by, among other necessities in the three additional drawers.

A stainless steel counter punctuates creamy cabinet bases. Here, a bookshelf extends out over the L-shaped counter.

Aquas, turquoises and blues are created in the shadows, crevices, and well-lit surfaces of this sea-blue kitchen. Azure blue with a white frost creates the mood.

Every corner is maximized. The range top tucks neatly under a corner vent hood. Full overlay doors allow for easy access underneath.

A true island in a sea of blue, this angle reveals a wine rack and cooling unit, tiny drawers for compartmentalized storage, and extended bar counters at each end for informal dining. Small seashell carvings punctuate each corner.

A brilliant aerial blue is used in a kitchen of sunflower yellows, creamy taupes, and wood tones. A tile backsplash gives a Mexican-inspired feel to the palette. The compact center island is punctuated by a long shelf with fitted baskets, a center console with TV screen, and a prep sink.

Drawers galore organize the ladles, spatulas, and stirring spoons.

Terra cottas, pinks, and reds inspire an earthy, simple, cottage kitchen. Two islands work side by sie to put all of the activity at the forefront.

The cooking island stores recipes and the cooktop.

A built-in counter serves as a computer station, with a pull-out laptop tray and book cubbies along the wall. The day's work tucks away and bottles of spirits below convert the elevated desk into a perfectly practical entertaining bar.

A striped floor runner leads to the charming window seat that boasts storage below and to the side. The islands offer two workspaces, isolating the hot cooking area from the washing and preparing area, letting two work together without bumping elbows.

Unifying colors tie together the contemporary—a soft robin's-egg-colored cabinet of clean lines and sleek silver hardware—with the antique and ancient, such as this same-color plant pot and rustic tile backsplash.

Bold color choices like this one are within anyone's reach. Favorite pieces, like this homeowner's bright dish collection, inspire.

Traditional cherry base cabinets are accented by cream maple
wall cabinets finished with a "skirt" of molding.

Color pulls up a chair for little merry-makers around a cherry peninsula table.

Custom cabinetry, including a roll-top desk, plunges into deep blue with white frost. Rounding the corner, a purple wall introduces the adjoining room.

We Love White

This cheerful kitchen with adjoining dining room found a way to use lots of black *and* stay bright and cheerful: plenty of *white*. Contrasting beautifully, the fireplace, diamond-designed floor, black dining furniture and black countertop on the cooktop are much more striking against bright white cabinetry and lemon-yellow walls.

Deep drawers hold linens, large pots, and more.

Here, white is paired with black, stainless steel, and hardwood for a clean, transitional look. Glass-paned doors carry forward a cottage feel, while shiny black countertops and contemporary fixtures and range take to the future.

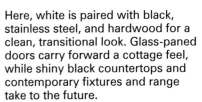

Roll-top cabinets for storing bread and appliances help keep those striking counters clutter-free.

A mini island is a great solution in this "U" work space.

Opposite page:
This gothic inspired kitchen is a charming take on an English cottage. Inset drawers and doors are surrounded by classic pilasters.

Above left:
Polka dots in white connect the walls to the cabinets in this fun kitchen. Perfectly round "dot" knobs show thoughtful planning in cabinet design.

Above:
From this angle, the farm sink with its bright, natural wood counter can be seen on the far wall, while a white marble counter adorns the island of custom cabinets and shelving.

Left:
In the corner, glass-front doors are uniquely lined with curtain-like fabric for a beautiful finish. A row of tiny, library-card-like drawers dots its way down to the floor, providing five distinct drawers for a kitchen's many gadgets.

Around the corner from a vast cooking library, large, double wall ovens are stacked above deep drawers and beside a dishwasher and sink of stainless steel.

Across the hardwood, a professional cooktop waits to fire up a meal for diners. A super-sized appliance garage is hidden behind a flip-up custom designed door.

Coffee and cream hues warm this space of tiny details and successful schemes that are set against a backdrop of sugar-white cabinets.

This built-in pantry masquerades as a freestanding furniture piece. The subtle set-back from the working kitchen adds custom architectural detail.

A gliding cabinet door rises to reveal an appliance garage that keeps clunkier gadgetry out of sight.

Rustic Recipes

Pull-outs upon pull-outs make storage simple and secret, sliding gracefully back into a thin space beside the refrigerator.

Celebrating natural materials like maple, stone, and granite this space takes you on a modern mountain get-away without leaving home. Granite slabs in earthy hues accent wide expanses of cabinetry and top an island that boasts a sink and seating.

Light shines from without and within this pastoral space. Maple cabinetry in a linen finish are a wonderful foil for furniture-inspired functional work areas. Turned pedestals in frosted Maple and raised panel doors and drawers add a warm tone that complements the natural hewn ceiling beams.

Open your cabinet and smell the coffee! This clever and compact appliance garage conceals behind country charm an otherwise contemporary-looking stainless device.

Drawers and doors in antique linen give the look of a cherished antique. A vertical plate rack holds dinner dishes tucked neatly under a custom nook surrounded by delicate peek-a-boo glass fronted cabinets.

89

A stacked stone backsplash and rust-and-stone-colored tile floor bring in the earthy colors of the West, and an artistic skull inspires an organic aire.

This "saddle chic" kitchen was designed to entertain. Double wine coolers, topped by glass fronted barware cabinets, make an efficient one-stop statement.

It doesn't get any more rustic than a wood-fired oven of gray stone emerging from a kitchen's corner. A granite counter echoes the oven's colors and spreads the charm across the tops of two-tone wood cabinetry. An antler chandelier ties the look together.

A tucked-in wet bar with bar taps and wine cooler gives this lodge-like corner of custom cabinetry. The welcome that makes an entertaining space warm.

Sticking to Tradition

This kitchen's multiple islands each boast a sink set into their warm brown granite counters. As evidenced by the spot that Spot has taken, stone tiles make a warm and welcoming floor surface for this space.

Classically traditional inset mortise and tenon doors and drawers topped by layered moldings and washed in a special latte-finish make this a truly custom kitchen.

Custom trim and molding details pull this sumptuous kitchen together. A large island features a prep sink and the ultimate in storage. Plate and wine racks make use of every nook and cranny..

Streamlined cabinetry makes the most of limited space. The simple "Tapestry" door adds a subtle detail to the clean lines. The cabinetry follows the architectural detailing of the bay window wall.

Beaded board wall finish is the perfect foil for the furniture-like look of the cabinetry. Built-in dresser drawers sit comfortably under an antique stained glass window.

With beaded inset doors, interior lighting, and open shelves this special wall cabinet is packed with flair and function.

Warm-ups and cool-downs are surrounded by Cherry in an heirloom stain. The wall ovens and refrigerator in stainless complement the cabinets, wine rack, and display cases. It's not far from cooktop to laptop thanks to a built-in kitchen office just across the way. It means business, from a desk decked in display cabinetry to deep filing drawers in matching cherry.

With the appearance of a freestanding heirloom, this elegant hutch features egg-and-dart moulding and a granite counter.

A delicately ornate, soft maple hutch offers a warm contrast to the wall and base cabinets in their low-sheen stain. A decorated vent hood arches over the stove and its tiled, fruit basket backsplash.

The fully integrated dishwasher is trimmed out in coordinating cabinetry panel and glass pull.

Tall and straight, this pull-out keeps spices at attention.

For a new spin on storage, this pie-cut corner cabinet rotates out of sight to get at the goodies stored on shelves

A window seat, with its mesh-fronted cabinets beneath, is "built-to-scale" in this cottage kitchen. Egg and dart molding surrounds the "wardrobe" in the corner.

This beauty takes "traditional" to unusual heights. In the kitchen, an island acts like a buffet fronting a breakfront of glass topped cabinets.

Pillars add a structural and design component to this classic space. Inset mortise and tenon cabinets on both sides of the island are the perfect solution for storing special occasion serve ware.

From this angle, the cook's secrets are revealed. A deep sink of stainless steel, a matching elegant dishwasher and a professional series stove fill the functional side of the "buffet."

Recessed spotlights in a tongue-and-groove paneled ceiling illuminate four columns that reach down to an island's high-gloss granite counter. A slate floor makes it simple to slide up a stool for an informal meal.

An adjoining prep area features suspended display cabinets, dishwasher and sink creating a stylish entertaining center.

Floor-to-ceiling cabinets with tall, glass-front doors act like freestanding china cabinets, offering an elegant option for extra storage.

This kitchen's double-bowl sink centers this Georgian design. Balanced from top to bottom, two rows of drawers surround the large undersink storage cabinets. Topped off by two rows of mini apothecary drawers and a center plate cabinet, this kitchen is at home in a classic architectural way.

A charming arch over the cooktop is the focal point of this traditional kitchen. Natural Cherry gives this elegant built-in kitchen extra panache.

Left:
Custom cabinetry continues into the dining room, where tiny pockets and drawers keep candlesticks, linens and fine flatware within reach. A simple horizontal wine rack rests under cabinets filled with stemware.

Right:
Double wall ovens are stacked for more compact presentation, a TV resides in a specially designed console and the microwave is tucked above a mini prep counter.

This Greek revival inspired space features a range hood designed to display. The built-in pot rack allows for easy access to sauté pans. The open, under-range shelving is a boon for large stew pots and mixing bowls.

An elegant built-in wine cooler is trimmed out in a chocolate stain with a white frost.

Unique shelf baskets hide produce under the counter. The corner prep sink is close by for quick scrubbing before heading to the soup pot.

This new take on tradition introduces a mini "baker" center on and in the island. A classic butler's pantry extends beyond the work space. Custom blue interiors set off collections of cream ware.

A classic southern summer kitchen, this pastel beauty introduces modern conveniences to an historic home. A new island designed to look old complements a new refrigerator trimmed out in hammered tin and coordinated wood finish.

This kitchen of deep, rich browns and navy blues makes efficient use of a small space with bar-height. At a deep island with cooktop, copper pots hang from a custom coordinated rack.

An antique finish known as brush mark crackle, is seen up close on the curve of a corner korbel.

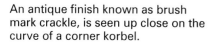

The built-in "town" breakfront features a classic Greek molding in inset drawers and doors. Complemented by the "country" side of upper and lower blue and white brush mark crackle cabinets.

Opposite page:
A plate rack tops a pretty sink with bronze finished fixtures. Beaded board backs the new yet old looking hutch.

Every detail was considered in this enormous kitchen. At the highest point, crown molding in off-white transitions the ceiling to the tall cabinets, where interior-lit glass-paned cabinets show off precious dishes and heirlooms. Below, the double-door refrigerator is hidden by a coordinating set of trim panels. Hovering above the super sized professional range is a coordinating custom panel range hood.

A second sink and pass through with additional informal seating and more incredible cabinets divides the kitchen from the living space.

A warming tray beneath the microwave and spice drawer keeps hot meals bubbling while diners are called to the kitchen.

An adjacent butler's pantry features a wine cooler and ice maker trimmed in coordinating Maple in a butter cream finish.

Bars and Beverage Stations

Warm on the outside and chilly on the inside, this icemaker sits cozily under the counter behind a cherry trim panel.

Glass fronts wood and wood fronts glass in this custom cabinet set that provides both on-display *and* discreet stemware storage.

Verde and black granite offers a counterpoint to the island and perimeter cabinetry, with a backsplash on the bias for added visual interest. Silvery door and drawer pulls smartly punctuate the cabinets, and a copper faucet makes a bold statement. Above, leaded glass panes provide a focal point.

This beverage center is a beauty. Two glass-front doors stand atop a custom wine storage cabinet, showing off stemware through glass paned doors.

Professsional wine cooler with temperature control holds vintage bottles behind a glass-front door. Beside it, stemware and other bottles are paired in layers for visual interest.

For the coffee connoisseur who expects more than the average Joe, this electric espresso maker is tucked into its very own spot among deep cherry cabinets. Just below it, a perfectly partitioned drawer keeps tiny espresso cups, fine grounds, and shakers of cinnamon and cocoa powder on hand for a rich, frothy pick-me-up.

This mountain cabin retreat kitchen offers classically chic storage for casual entertaining.

Other Rooms

An armoire perfect for this active, outdoorsy family boasts a built-in bench for tying up waders, hooks for dangling the fishing net and dog leash within easy reach, and a tiny den below for man's best friend.

A mudroom doubles as laundry center and garden room.

Just off the kitchen, custom cabinetry conceals a stacking washer and dryer. Jackets, scarves, hats and gloves are tucked away behind mudroom "closet" doors.

The Butler's Pantry is a great workspace for caterers, and provides storage for special-occasion cooking and serving wares.

This potting center provides style, storage, and sink space for the avid gardener.

Custom cabinetry flanks a vanity, so that a fluffy, clean towel is always at hand. Casters below make it easy to maintain dust-free floors and a spotless sink, by just wheeling aside the storage units and deep-cleaning.

Dual-tone cabinetry creates a pretty horizontal line in this custom bath with vessel sinks.

Many thanks to all of the participating Plain & Fancy dealers of true custom cabinetry.

We owe a debt of gratitude to our dealers whose kitchen installations are featured in this Plain & Fancy Custom Cabinetry 40th Anniversary commemorative book. And to all of our dealers who have helped homeowners make Plain & Fancy their one and only.

Allen Cabinets, Pequannock, NJ
American Kitchens, Charlotte, NC
Artisan Kitchens & Baths, Fairfax Station, VA

Bolyard Lumber Company, Rochester, MI
Burgin Kitchens, Commerce Township, MI

Cabinet Concepts, Inc., Marquette, MI
Cove Station Kitchens, James Creek, PA
Cranbury Design Center, Hightstown, NJ
Creative Kitchen and Bath, Merritt, NC

Design Solutions, Newark, DE
Dovetailed Kitchens of Manchester, Manchester, NH

Eldredge Lumber & Hardware, York, ME
Empire Bath & Kitchen, Utica, NY

F.A. McGonegal, Falls Church, VA
Fingerle Lumber Co., Ann Arbor, MI
Front Row Kitchens and Baths, Norwalk, CT

Granite State, Bedford, NH

J & L Kitchen and Baths, Milburn, NJ

Kitchen & Bath Design Center, Bantam, CT
Kitchen & Bath Design Consultants, West Hartford, CT
Kitchen Interiors, Natick, MA
Kitchen Traditions, Danbury, CT
Kitchen Visions, Columbia, SC
Kitchens By Design, Allentown, PA
Kitchens By Stephanie, Grand Rapids, MI
Kitchens by Turano, Nutley, NJ

LaFollette Kitchen & Bath, Williamstown, MI
Lakeville Industries, Inc., Lindenhurst, NY
Laura Marr Baur Interior Designs, Dexter, MI

Laurie Wallace Design, Bloomington, IL
Luv My Kitchen, Miami Beach, FL

Maine Kitchen Design, Yarmouth, MA
Majestic, Mamaroneck, NY
Maldon Cabinetry, Ridgefield, CT
Midatlantic Custom Building Group, Gambrills, MD
Mill Valley Kitchens, Baltimore, MD
Millwork Masters, Ltd., Keene, NH
Miters Touch, Boone, NC
Montague Branch Cabinetry, Alexandria, VA
Montauk Woodworks, Montauk, NY
Morgan House Interiors, Clinton, NJ

Nassau Suffolk Lumber & Supply, Ronkonkome, NY
New Look Kitchens & Baths, Front Royal, VA
Normandy Construction, Hinsdale, IL

Oread Design, Vandergift, PA

Pillsbury's, Kennebunk, ME
Pittam Associates, Atlanta GA
Plain & Fancy Design Center, Schaefferstown, PA

Quintessentials, NYC, NY

Robinwood Kitchens, Berkeley Heights, NJ
Room Service, Stroudsburg, PA

S.W. Scheipeter Construction, Webster Groves, MO
Schuon Kitchens Inc., Roswell, GA
Sea Island Kitchens, Hilton Head Isle, SC
Stevenson Millwork, Fishkill, NY
Sticks and Stones, Boston, MA

The Cabinetry, Hanover, MA
The Cabinetworks, Stratham, NH
The Kitchen Center in Bridgeport Lumber, Bridgeport, CT
The Kitchen Co., Washington, DC

U.S. Kitchens and Baths, Hackettstown, NJ

Warren's Wood Works, Easton, MD

Photography on page 110 and 108 by Jennifer Jordan